Usborne

Big Picture Book
Outdoors

Minna Lacey

Illustrated by Rachel Stubbs
and John Russell

Designed by Lucy Wain

By the river

All kinds of birds and small creatures make their nests among the reeds and grasses that grow by rivers. Many feed on water plants, insects and small fish.

Reeds

chu chu chu chu
Song thrush

cheep
Ducklings learning to swim
quack
cheep cheep
Ducks

Chaffinch

buzzzzzizz
Bumblebee

A mother duck sits on her eggs for up to 30 days, until they're ready to hatch.

Water vole

Little egret

Goose

honk honk

Lots of water birds have wide, webbed feet to paddle fast through the water.

Butterfly

Ladybird

Rabbit

zerrr tee-tee-tee
Wren

Moth

Swallows
dart through the air, then swoop low to chase flying insects over the water.

A duck comes in to land on the water.

Willow tree.

Pike
A giant pike hunts small fish just below the surface.

SPLISH SPLASH

Kingfisher
Kingfishers dive underwater to catch fish and frogs.

Great crested grebe
The chicks of some water birds ride on their parents' backs.

Fish leap out of the water to swallow flies.

Bulrushes

Water lilies

Damselflies
need sunshine to warm up their bodies, to give them enough energy to fly.

squawk

Coot

Heron
Herons use their long, sharp beaks to snap up fish.

Otters
A family of otters rests on the bank. Otters make their home, called a holt, among the roots of trees.

Wild flowers

You can find wild flowers growing in meadows, by the edges of fields and in clearings in the middle of woods. Look out for them in other places too – on roadsides, by railways, in ditches and on wasteland.

White bell-shaped flowers

Petals curl out at the ends.

Wild strawberries

Five white petals

Flower bud

Fruit

Lily of the valley

Two leaves grow from the base of plant.

Bluebells

Foxgloves
have drooping funnel-shaped flowers, with dark spots inside.

Violets
have small, deep purple flowers with heart-shaped leaves.

These blue flowers often grow in woodlands and come out in the spring.

Wild roses
twist and climb over shrubs and trees in hedgerows and woodland clearings.

Cowslips

have groups of yellow flower heads that grow from a single tall stem.

These cup-shaped flowers come out in early spring.

Found in sunny, grassy meadows

Bee orchids

These flowers look like female bees. This attracts male bees. When bees visit flowers, they spread a powder called pollen, which helps flowers make fruit and seeds.

Large red, overlapping petals

Poppies

often grow around corn fields.

Bud

Daisies

have long white petals surrounding a circle of tiny yellow petals, known as the 'eye'.

Buttercups

are common in fields and river meadows.

Shiny golden petals

Fields

Rooks
fly across the fields in large flocks at dusk...
...and nest together in trees.

The clump of trees where they nest is called a rookery.

caw caw caw

Cuckoo *cuckoo cuckoo*

Hedgerows
are made of bushy plants and wild flowers.

Deer often eat the bark of young trees.

Fallow deer

Grass snake

Partridge

Rabbits
come out at dawn and dusk to nibble fresh, young shoots.

Woodpecker
Green woodpeckers often look for ants on the ground.

Fox
Foxes stalk through the grass, hunting small animals and birds.

Weasels

Mole
This creature has wide front paws shaped like spades to dig tunnels.

Tree roots

Rabbits live under the ground in a network of burrows called a warren.

Young rabbits are called kittens.

Hedgerows

Many fields are bordered by hedgerows, where lots of animals can feed, shelter and nest.

Ivy flowers make lots of nectar, a sweet juice that bees use to make honey.

Ivy

squeak
squeak
squeak

Wood mouse
Wood mice gather seeds, berries, nuts and insects. They store them in burrows underground.

Caterpillar
Many caterpillars feed on ivy leaves, berries or buds.

Blackberries
are prickly climbing plants. They produce dark, juicy berries in the autumn.

zzzzzzzzzz

Wasp

Greenfinch
These birds crack open nuts and seeds with their strong, thick beaks.

Hoverfly

Comma butterfly

Cow parsley

Honeysuckle

Ladybirds
crawl over plants eating tiny insects, called aphids.

Aphids

Stag beetle
Male stag beetles fight each other using large antler-shaped jaws.

bzzzzz

Honey bee
Bees eat nectar and a yellow powder in flowers called pollen.

Sea and cliffs

On the coast, you can see a huge number of seabirds, huddling together on rocks, screeching from cliffs and diving into the sea for fish.

Kyyaaaa kyyaaaa

Lighthouse
A lighthouse shines a strong beam of light at night to warn ships away from dangerous rocks.

Oil tanker

PSSSHHH

Fin whale

Cave

Over thousands of years, the waves carve holes in the rocks.

Fishing boat

Basking shark
These huge fish swim slowly near the surface, eating tiny plants and creatures called plankton.

Dolphins

Kittiwake and chicks

Wild flowers grow on top of the cliffs.

Many seabirds build their nests on narrow ledges in the cliffs.

Sea campion

Notice the orange tips.

Orange tip butterfly

Six-spot burnet moth

Kyyaaaa kyyaaaa

Gulls
High over the cliffs, gulls swoop, turn and soar in the sea breeze.

Herring gull

Diving birds, like this gannet, spot fish in the sea from high above the water.

Puffins
live out at sea for most of the year. They only come to land to nest and bring up their young.

Gannet

Seals

Some plants by the sea have thick fleshy stems that hold water, so they don't dry out in the wind.

Wheatear

Puffins nest in burrows on the cliff tops. Each mother bird lays just one egg.

Rock samphire
grows in rocky places.

Sea pink

Crane fly

Crab spider

Ants

Looking at birds

Different types of birds have different shaped bodies, beaks and feet. You can also recognize birds by looking at their markings – or by listening to the calls they make.

To identify a bird, it helps to be able to describe its main body parts.

Tail

Crown

Wing

Feet

Bill or beak

Breast

Belly

Wren

Wing feathers fan out to help birds balance and fly.

House sparrow

This bird has a thin, sharp bill for snapping up insects mid-air.

Spotted flycatcher

Kestrel
Hunting birds have strong claws, called talons, for clutching and tearing their prey.

Coot

A coot is a water bird with big, wide feet for walking on soft mud.

Treecreeper
Curved gripping claws help this bird walk up, down and sideways on trees.

Shoveler
This duck has a huge flat bill to skim the water for food.

Cormorant
Cormorants have long necks and hooked bills for catching fish.

Avocet

This bird's upturned beak helps it sift through mud for creatures to eat.

Chaffinch
Male chaffinches have pinky red bodies and white stripes on their wings.

Blue tit
Black eye stripe

Blue crown

Blue wings

purrrrrrrrr purrrrr

Turtle doves

Song thrush

chu chu chu dee dee dee

If you listen carefully outdoors, you might hear birds even if you can't see them.

A song thrush has a beautiful song, made up of different calls repeated three or four times.

Tawny owl

hoooooooooooo hoo hoo hoo

drr drr drr

Great spotted woodpecker
Woodpeckers make a fast drumming sound as they drill into trees with their strong bills.

Rock pools

cour-lee cour-lee

Curlew

Periwinkles
are small sea snails.

Mussels

Cockles

Ringed plover

tooo-eee

SPLASH

Shorebirds scurry across the sand, picking out worms and snails.

When the tide goes out, all kinds of sea creatures are left behind in rocky pools on the seashore.

Crab

Pipefish
suck up small fish with their long snouts.

Cowrie shell

Blenny

Hermit crabs
make their homes inside empty shells.

Egg cases

Sea anemones
are creatures that catch fish and shrimp with sticky tentacles.

Sharks and rays lay eggs in cases, sometimes called mermaids' purses, which get washed in by the tide.

Goby

Barnacles
open up in water to catch tiny plants and animals to eat.

Yacht

kee-arrr kee-arrr

Terns

Oystercatcher
This seabird opens shells with its
long bill to eat the animals inside.

Many sea creatures live
inside shells. They attach
themselves to rocks so they
don't get washed away
by the waves.

Prrrr rrp

snap snap snap

Cuttlefish bone

Limpets
cling tightly onto rocks when
they're out of the water.

Cuttlefish

But underwater,
limpets move about
eating seaweed.

Seaweed

Shrimp

Scallops

Sea urchins
are protected inside
a spiky shell.

Razor
shell

Starfish

Whelks

Starfish grip onto
rocks using small
suckers under
their arms.

Trees

Many trees grow tall and wide – and some can live for a thousand years. Their leaves, branches and trunks provide a home and food for hundreds of insects, birds and small creatures.

The top layer of branches and leaves is called the canopy.

Trees that are green all year round are called 'evergreen'.

Trees need food to grow. They use sunlight to make it in their leaves.

A layer of tough bark protects the trunk.

Birds look for beetles and grubs under leaves and inside the bark.

Trees, like this one, that lose their leaves in winter, are called 'deciduous'.

Trees suck up water from the soil through their roots.

Leaves

One of the best ways to recognize trees is by the shape of their leaves.

Lime
Smooth, heart-shaped leaves

Larch
Soft, needle-like leaves

Oak
Small leaves with wavy edges

Yew
Dark green needles that grow in rows

Field maple
The sap or liquid in maple trees is used to make maple syrup.

Food and water travel through tubes called veins.

Silver birch
Oval pointed leaves with jagged edges

Ash
Lots of small leaflets grow from a single stem.

Leaflet

Stem

Horse chestnut
These leaflets look a little like fingers on a hand.

Holly
Smooth, waxy leaves with spiky edges

Things to spot

There are all sorts of things you can look out for outdoors – fruit, seeds, feathers or animal tracks – that tell you about the animals and plants nearby.

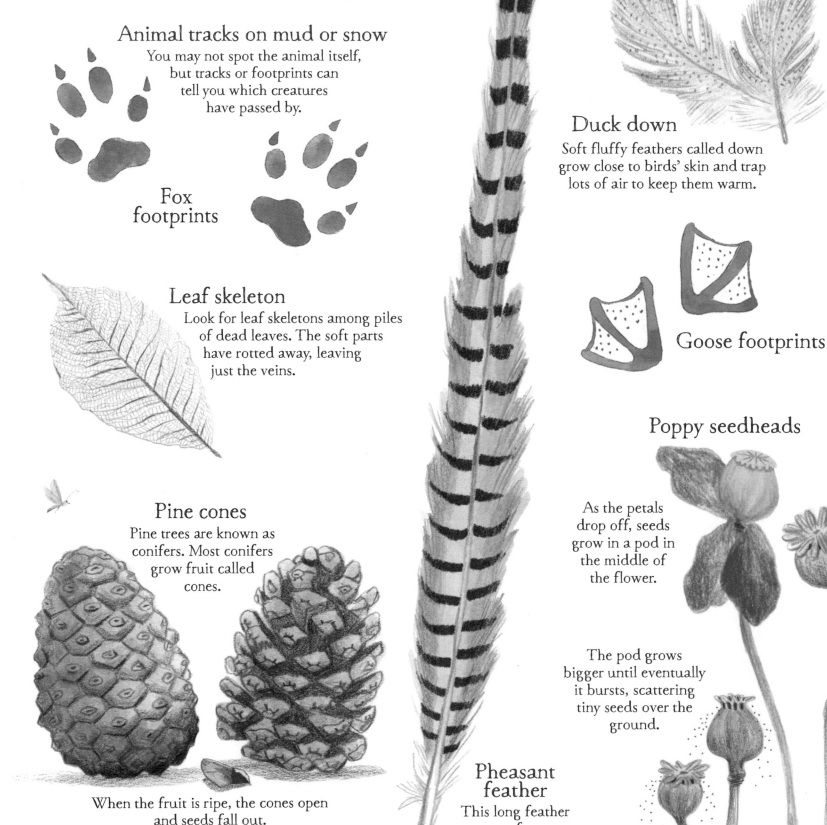

Animal tracks on mud or snow

You may not spot the animal itself, but tracks or footprints can tell you which creatures have passed by.

Fox footprints

Leaf skeleton

Look for leaf skeletons among piles of dead leaves. The soft parts have rotted away, leaving just the veins.

Pine cones

Pine trees are known as conifers. Most conifers grow fruit called cones.

When the fruit is ripe, the cones open and seeds fall out.

Pine seed

Birds regularly lose worn-out feathers, and grow new ones.

Duck down

Soft fluffy feathers called down grow close to birds' skin and trap lots of air to keep them warm.

Goose footprints

Poppy seedheads

As the petals drop off, seeds grow in a pod in the middle of the flower.

The pod grows bigger until eventually it bursts, scattering tiny seeds over the ground.

Pheasant feather

This long feather comes from a pheasant's tail.

Sycamore seeds
Sycamore seeds are light and papery and shaped like wings, that spin through the air.

Horse chestnut fruit
When the spiky fruit is ripe, it splits to reveal round, shiny seeds, called conkers.

Deer hoofprints

Squirrel footprints

Apple
Apple seeds are protected inside the fruit's fleshy core.

Miner marks
The pale squiggles on this leaf are tunnels made by a tiny caterpillar called a leaf miner.

Wood pigeon feather
This strong, stiff feather comes from a pigeon's wing.

Tree rings
You can see rings on tree stumps. Each year tree wood grows a new ring. If you count them, you can find out the tree's age.

Wide rings show the years when the tree grew a lot.

Teasel
This spiny seed head is like a brush. Its seeds attract lots of birds in winter.

Pondlife

screeee screeee screeee
Swifts

Small birds perch on reeds, looking for insects.

Yellow irises

Mayflies
Newly hatched mayflies swarm over the water.

Moorhens and chicks

peep peep peep peep

Frog
Every spring, frogs come to ponds to mate and lay eggs.

Water spiders
live underwater, but need air to breathe. So they trap air bubbles in their body hairs.

Waterboatman
This bug paddles near the surface with long back legs, like oars.

Tench

Crayfish

Newts

Tadpoles
hatch from frogs' eggs. After several weeks, the tadpoles turn into frogs.

Water beetles

Water plants make oxygen, which fish use to breathe.

Hobby
This bird swoops over ponds and rivers to catch dragonflies in mid-air.

Bulrushes
A mouse peeps out from the reeds.

squeak

BOOM BOOM BOOM

Bittern
This bird lives among the reeds. It makes a deep call like a ship's horn.

Grass snake
These are often found near water. They swim across ponds to hunt frogs and newts.

Pond skaters
are so light, they can slide across the water's surface.

Water shrew

Dragonfly young are called nymphs. They can live underwater for more than a year before they turn into dragonflies.

Water scorpion
This bug grasps tadpoles and tiny fish in its front legs and sucks out their juices.

Water shrews dive to hunt for shrimp, fish eggs and small fish.

Pond snail

Stickleback

City ramble

You can spot wildlife in all sorts of unexpected places around towns and cities – by the side of canals or railway lines, and in parks and gardens.

Peregrine falcon
These are the fastest animals in the world. You may see them nesting at the top of tall buildings or flying at high speed.

Look out for birds perching on posts or telephone wires.

Sparrow

Starling

Pigeon

Buttercups

Many wild plants and flowers grow well on poor or rough ground.

Rat

Dandelion

Magpie
Magpies have striking black and white feathers and a chattering call.

chakker chakkerrr

Buddleia
is also known as the butterfly bush, because its flowers attract so many butterflies.

Peacock butterfly

Jay

Small white butterfly

Fox

Foxes creep about in quiet streets, gardens and on disused land.

Mouse

Shrew

Grey squirrel

Stag beetle

Woodland wildlife

In woodlands, trees grow close together, creating shade and cover for lots of animals. Branches, leaves or pine needles fall to the ground and rot, making food for millions of insects and bugs.

Nuthatches
climb up and down trunks and branches, picking out insects and seeds.

Ink cap mushrooms

Peacock butterfly

Nettles
grow in woodland clearings. Many butterflies lay eggs on them for their caterpillars to feed on.

Crossbill
These birds have X-shaped bills to help them open pine cones and pull out the seeds.

Millipede
Millipedes have long bodies and lots of legs.

Wood anemone
White flowers come out in spring.

Adder or viper
These snakes have zigzag markings and live in open woodland, moors and meadows.

Wild garlic
These white star-like flowers come out in early spring. The leaves and flowers smell of garlic.

Red squirrel

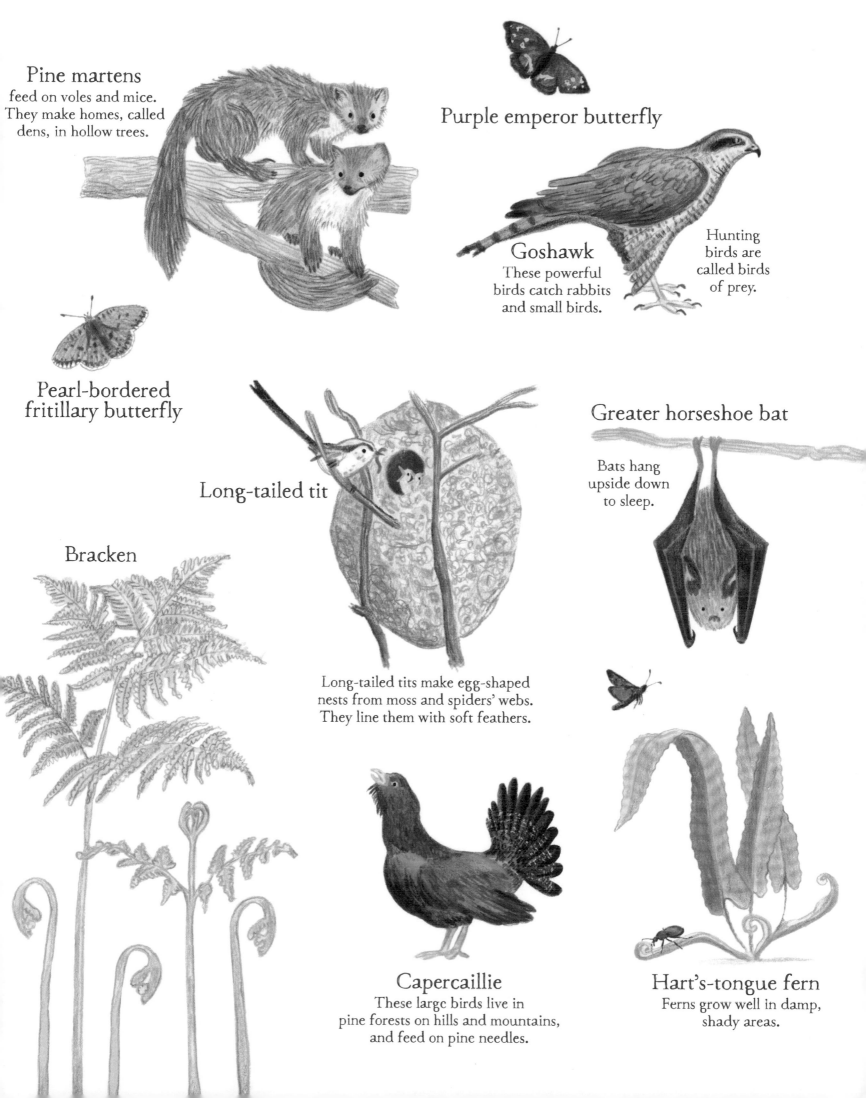

Pine martens
feed on voles and mice.
They make homes, called
dens, in hollow trees.

Purple emperor butterfly

Goshawk
These powerful
birds catch rabbits
and small birds.

Hunting
birds are
called birds
of prey.

**Pearl-bordered
fritillary butterfly**

Long-tailed tit

Greater horseshoe bat

Bats hang
upside down
to sleep.

Bracken

Long-tailed tits make egg-shaped
nests from moss and spiders' webs.
They line them with soft feathers.

Capercaillie
These large birds live in
pine forests on hills and mountains,
and feed on pine needles.

Hart's-tongue fern
Ferns grow well in damp,
shady areas.

Four seasons

Spring

Fresh, green leaves unfurl on trees, flowers burst into bloom and the sound of birdsong fills the air.

toot

tra laa lee tra

Summer

As it grows warmer, insects buzz and meadows fill with flowers, while many animals feed and care for their young.

Trees are covered in leaves.

Crops ripen in the fields.

After building a nest, birds lay eggs then keep them warm until they are ready to hatch.

Trees, such as hazel and silver birch, have long hanging flowers, called catkins.

Sheep

Lambs

Butterflies fly from flower to flower drinking nectar.

Many animals give birth to their young in the spring.

As the ground grows warmer, new seedlings push through the soil.

Caterpillars

Daffodils

Hedgehog

Lizard

Reptiles, like this lizard, bask in the early morning sunshine.

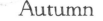

Autumn

Fruit and berries ripen, while leaves on
many trees turn yellow and orange
before they fall to the ground.

Winter

The temperature drops and snow may fall in
some areas. Ponds may freeze and some animals
fall into a deep sleep called hibernation.

Kestrel

Snowman

Apple tree

Snowflake

Icicles
form when
dripping water
freezes.

Squirrel

Squirrels collect nuts and
bury them in the ground,
to store for the winter.

Ice forms on the
top layer of ponds
and lakes.

Mushrooms

Mountain hare

Some animals grow
white fur in winter so
they blend in with
the snow.

Robin

Dandelions

make hundreds of
tiny, white seeds that
spread in the wind.

Duck

Spider
and web

Footprints
in the snow

Dormouse

Fox

High in the hills

Golden eagle
These huge birds soar over mountains and hills, often lifting their wings in a wide V shape.

moooooo

baa

Highland cattle
have two layers of long, thick hair to keep them warm in cold winds and heavy rain.

Heather

Mountain hare
These animals have brown fur in summer, but turn white in winter, if it's very cold and the hills are covered in snow.

Cottongrass
flowers look like cotton balls.

Red grouse

Osprey
This bird has caught a fish with its sharp talons.

Heather in flower looks like a purple carpet over hills and moors.

Red deer
Female red deer, called hinds, live in a herd with their young.

Male deer, called stags, grow antlers with up to 16 points. Their antlers drop off and grow again each year.

baaaaa

Sheep
Blackface sheep have very curly horns. They climb rocky hillsides and survive in icy weather.

Male sheep, called rams, fight by clashing horns until one backs down.

Meadow pipit
Meadow pipits look for insects and spiders living in the bracken.

Wildcat
This wildcat pads silently through the bushes, hunting mice and voles.

glug-glug-glug-glug

Gorse

Grouse make low glug-glug sounds in the long grass.

Vole

Caterpillars and butterflies

From tiny eggs, butterflies go through amazing
changes, before turning into their adult shape.

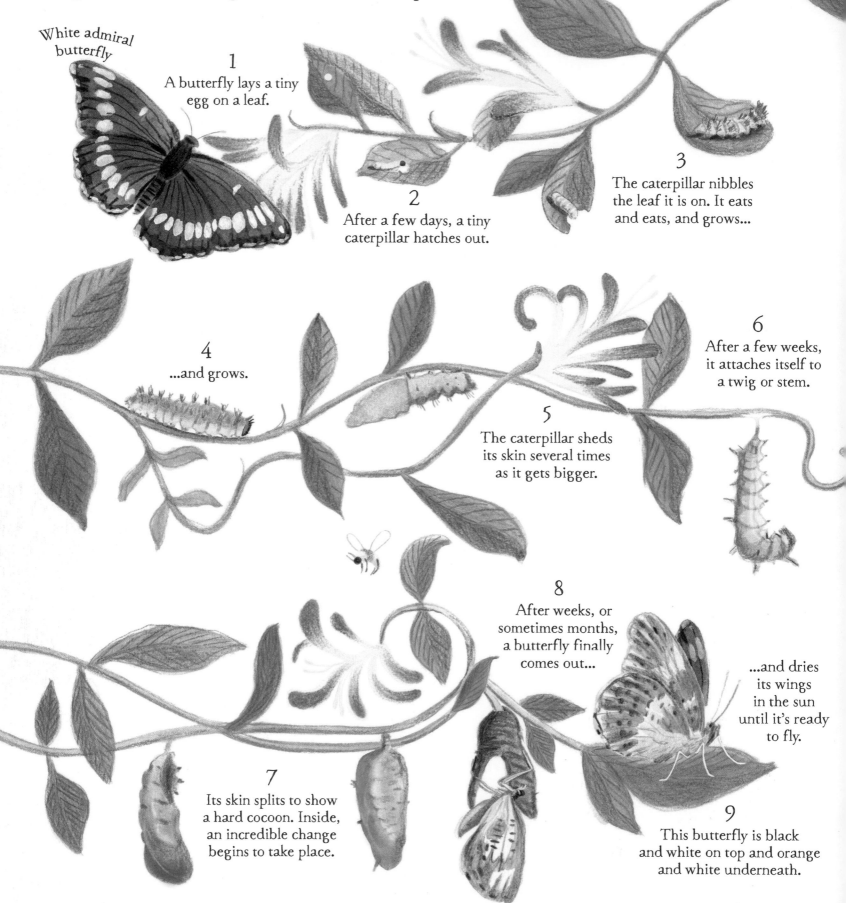

White admiral
butterfly

1
A butterfly lays a tiny
egg on a leaf.

2
After a few days, a tiny
caterpillar hatches out.

3
The caterpillar nibbles
the leaf it is on. It eats
and eats, and grows...

4
...and grows.

5
The caterpillar sheds
its skin several times
as it gets bigger.

6
After a few weeks,
it attaches itself to
a twig or stem.

7
Its skin splits to show
a hard cocoon. Inside,
an incredible change
begins to take place.

8
After weeks, or
sometimes months,
a butterfly finally
comes out...

...and dries
its wings
in the sun
until it's ready
to fly.

9
This butterfly is black
and white on top and orange
and white underneath.

Tadpoles and frogs

Frogs go through many changes of shape, too.

1
A female frog lays thousands of eggs, called frogspawn, near the surface of ponds and lakes.

2
Each egg looks like a tiny black dot in a blob of gel.

3
Each black dot grows into a tadpole that wriggles and wriggles inside the gel.

4
After several days, if the water is warm enough, the tadpoles eat the gel and hatch out.

5
They feed on plants and tiny creatures, and grow bigger...

6
...and bigger.

7
When they're 6-9 weeks old, they grow two back legs.

8
They start to look more like frogs – but they still have tails.

9
At around 12 weeks, their tails drop off. They're now tiny, fully-formed frogs.

After dark

Many creatures stay hidden during the day and come out at night. They're known as nocturnal animals.

Barn owl
Owls have special wing feathers to help them fly silently over fields, hunting mice and voles.

Moon

Hay barn

Fallow deer

Deer often leave safer woodland areas at night to browse in open fields.

Moths

Lapwing

Many flowers, such as honeysuckle, give out a strong scent in the evening that attracts moths.

Snail

Slug

Bat

Bats make high clicks and squeaks that bounce back off things. This helps them find their way in the dark.

Nightjar

This night-flying bird chases moths in woodland clearings.

Tawny owl and chicks

Owl chicks, called owlets, climb out of their nest before they learn to fly.

Badgers come out to feed at dusk. The cubs leap and play near their tunnel home, which is called a sett.

Cubs

Badger

croak croak croak

Toad

During the day, toads hide under leaves or logs. At night, they come out to look for insects, slugs and worms.

snuffle snuffle snuffle

Hedgehog

These animals have over 5,000 spines on their bodies, to protect them from other animals attacking.

Internet links

To find out more about wildlife and lots of
nature activities you can do outdoors, go to
www.usborne.com/quicklinks and type in the
keywords 'big picture book outdoors'.

Expert advice from
Tim Dee

Series editor: Ruth Brocklehurst   Managing designer: Nicola Butler